LIVING WITH TYPE 1 DIABETES

Philip PATMAN

Important Healthcare Disclaimer

This illustrated book for children is provided for educational and informational purposes only and does not constitute providing medical advice or professional services. The information provided should not be used for diagnosing or treating a health problem or disease, and those seeking personal medical advice should consult with a licensed physician. Always seek the advice of your doctor or other qualified health provider regarding a medical condition. Never disregard professional medical advice or delay in seeking it because of something you have read here. If you think you may have a medical emergency, call local emergency number or go to the nearest emergency room immediately. No physician-patient relationship is created by this children illustrated book or its use. Neither the Publisher nor its employees, nor any contributor to this children illustrated book, makes any representations, express or implied, with respect to the information provided herein or to its use

Without all of you, we could not have created this newest series of Ana and Tomy the Superkids. your support helped us ensure that this book contains the latest and most accurate information possible, information that answers today's kids questions and concerns about their health, their personal hygiene, diseases and illnesses. Thank you for your comments and thank you for supporting our initiative for the good of our kids. THANK YOU!

Tim and Francesca Harrison
Anne-Marthe Moudouthe
Ndabo Diyouckey Hélène
Laurence Mandengue
Franck Beltrami
Danielle F. Balem
Eric Epassa
Jean Georges Ngatsimi
Pamela Njowe Ndongue
Gerard Philip Mbouyap
Diane Bita Minsili
Anne Ngu
Philomene Gaelle
Joanne Emilie Mbella
Bintu Dell
Benedicte M. Mandengue
Esther Epouner
Fawziya Atintande
Yannick Menye Ndzana
John Mpapa Munanga
Yvette Michele Mendo'o
Vanessa and Patrick N.
Alice Ebenye
Junang Nono
Vicky Piau
Fotemah Mba
Fred Nono
Willy Nelle
Steve Dengoue
Viviane Belomo
Jean Junior Tigyo
Gerard Eyidi

Julien Ngue
Stephane Balogue
Marc-Eric Ngoundo Black
Friedman Tchoffo Talom
Pascale Balem
Sadissa Babeni
Yohan Bita Minsili
Olivia Ondoua Sanga
Mounia Aram
Yannick Eko
Dora Helene Eboa
Yannick Mengue
Elise Edimo
Brigitte Kanko Atangana
Babeth Kembelol
Olivier Foti
Gabriel Betenye
Ato Micah
Victorine Epesse
Sarah Dinene Divine-Garba
Lydienne Locko
Bernard Banamba
Nara Monkam
H. Patricia Bitond
Blaise Mounga
Nathalie Tagni
Spagnolo-Ndoumbe Anne
Reine Dibussi
Jean Junior TIGYO
Frank Mitambo
Reine Ntone Johansen
Julien Ngue
Thierry Ebata
Hannelore Ebongue
Tecla Mbongue
Franscica Irma
Kalinka Essome
Letricia Njoh
Martial Miamo
Edgar Francis Datchoua
Stephane Nieniel
Lydienne Locko-Fotsing
Christian Minoue
Noel Nyamsi
Patrick Epee
Rosinne Ntienjem
Christelle Wandji
Kelly White Kell

To my kids, Wellysane, Ywaika and Janea, remember that: "Education is the most powerful weapon which you can use to change the world." -Nelson Mandela

Living with Type1 Diabetes
A children book with Ana and Tomy The Superkids
Published by The SuperKids Adventures Books
www.TheSuperkidsBooks.com

Book designs by Delphine M. Shooter and brgfx / Freepik

THE SUPERKIDS ADVENTURES BOOKS

All inquiries of this book can be sent to the author:
K502 Brakwatso Street App 2 Adjiringanor, Accra – Ghana
Tel: +233 506 679 679
Email: philip.patman@thesuperkidsbooks.com

UNITED BOOKS
FOR CHILDREN

INTRODUCING
ANA & TOMY THE SUPERKIDS

ANA

Ana is the main character. She is a no-nonsense, straightforward kid. She is also very sharp and she wants everybody to know that. Not very humble, right?

TOMY

Tomy is Ana's twin brother. He's fun loving, friendly, easy going and adventurous. He likes to play with his watergun and calls his toys **Atomic**. Guess why?

Mrs. KAREN

Mrs. Karen is the School nurse. She is also Ana and Tomy mother.She helps them to understand the illnesses and the germs

TERRY

Terry aka ***The Terror***, is a well known bully at school. He is always dirty and very vengeful.

RUSS

Russ is Terry's best friend. He is violent, slow and likes to eat. He is not very smart.

FUNGUY

Funguy is a clown, and a prankster. He is also Ana and Tomy's cousin.

ZOE

Zoe is Russ' sister. She is always dark and gothic. She likes her pet reptiles more than people.

With Mr. FIELDS

The Physical Education (PE) teacher

Ana and Tomy are siblings who struggle against school bullies Terry and his gang (Russ, Funguy and Zoe) but enjoy fighting their alter ego as germs inside the bodies of their infected classmates. Ana & Tomy - The SuperKids is a medical series to learn and improve child Mental and Body health.

SUPER ANA

Super Ana is the Superkid version of Ana. She is sharp and smart . She finds the right solutions inside the body to fight the germs.

SUPER TOMY

Super Tomy is the Superkid version of Tomy. He is in charge of the logistics: The Superjet, the weapons and other ammunitions.

WHITE CELL

White blood cells are also called leukocytes. They protect you against illness and disease They flow through your bloodstream to fight viruses, bacteria, and other foreign invaders that threaten your health

BACTERIA

Bacteria are ubiquitous, mostly free-living organisms often consisting of one biological cell

VIRUS

Non-cellular, submicroscopic infectious agent that replicates only inside the living cells of an organism

FUNGUS

Fungi are eukaryotic organisms that, like algae, have rigid cell walls and may be either unicellular or multicellular

PROTOZOA

Protozoa are microscopic, one-celled organisms that can be free-living or parasitic in nature

Also Featuring Ryan

The main star of this book

The P.E. teacher was stretching with some children outside. Everybody was excited about the upcoming roller skate competition.

Kids were putting on their roller skates when Terry arrived with Russ and his sister Zoe.

Terry said: "**Little kids, let the champions pass!**"

Meanwhile, Tomy introduced Ryan to Ana.

"**Ana, this is Ryan. It's a good skater and he will be in our team**" Tomy said.

"**Hello Ana!**" Ryan said.

"**Hi Ryan! Welcome to our team.**" Ana replied.

Terry and his friends came to confront Ana and her team.

Terry said: "**Hey losers! We are here to win. We are the best roller skaters.**"

Tomy responded: "**No way! You can only win if you cheat.**"

The kids started to shout at each other.

Fortunately, the P.E. teacher came to separate them.

He told them: "**No fight, kids! You should show your skills on the racetrack instead.**"

Mr. Fields launched the qualification race.

Ready ... Set ... Go!

Terry, Russ, and Zoe won their race and qualified for the finals.

Ana, Tomy and Ryan also won their race and qualified for the finals.

At the canteen, the kids were taking their lunch.

Ana said: "**Ryan, slow down! You are eating too much.**"

"**...and too fast. You are going to choke your-self.**" Tomy added.

Ryan replied: "**Don't worry guys, I need a lot of energy...and I have a little secret.**"

Ryan's little Secret: He has **Type 1 Diabetes**

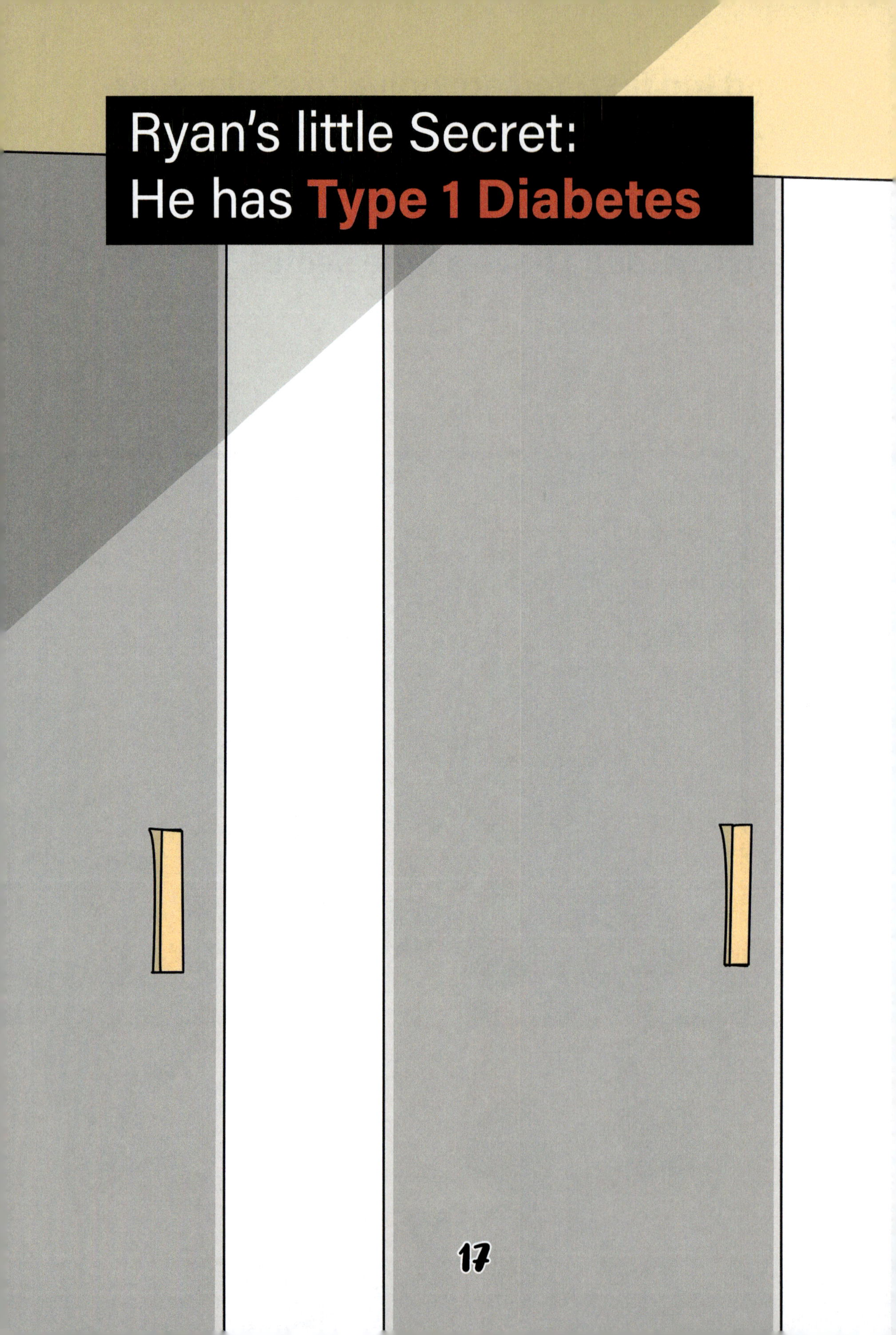

Funguy discovered Ryan's secret and went to reveal it to Terry and his friends

Funguy said:"**Guys, I know how you can win the race again Ana, Tomy and Ryan.**"

Later in the afternoon, Mr. Fields announced the 4 teams qualified for the final race.

He said:" **Congratulations to all of you! Now the qualified teams need to prepare for the final race. Good luck!**"

Terry and Russ met with Ryan on the hallway and offered him a sandwich.

"Hi Ryan, are you hungry? we brought you a sandwich." Russ said.

"Yes, I am. Thank you guys. Sandwiches are good for energy." Ryan replied.

At the same time, *Zoe stole Ryan's* **Insulin pen** *from his bag*.

During the warm-up before the final race, Ryan was weak and tired, and he fell on the ground.

Terry was very happy.

Mr. Fields, the P.E. Teacher, sent Ryan to the infirmary.

He said: " **This is very unfortunate for your team, Ana. Ryan is not well.**"

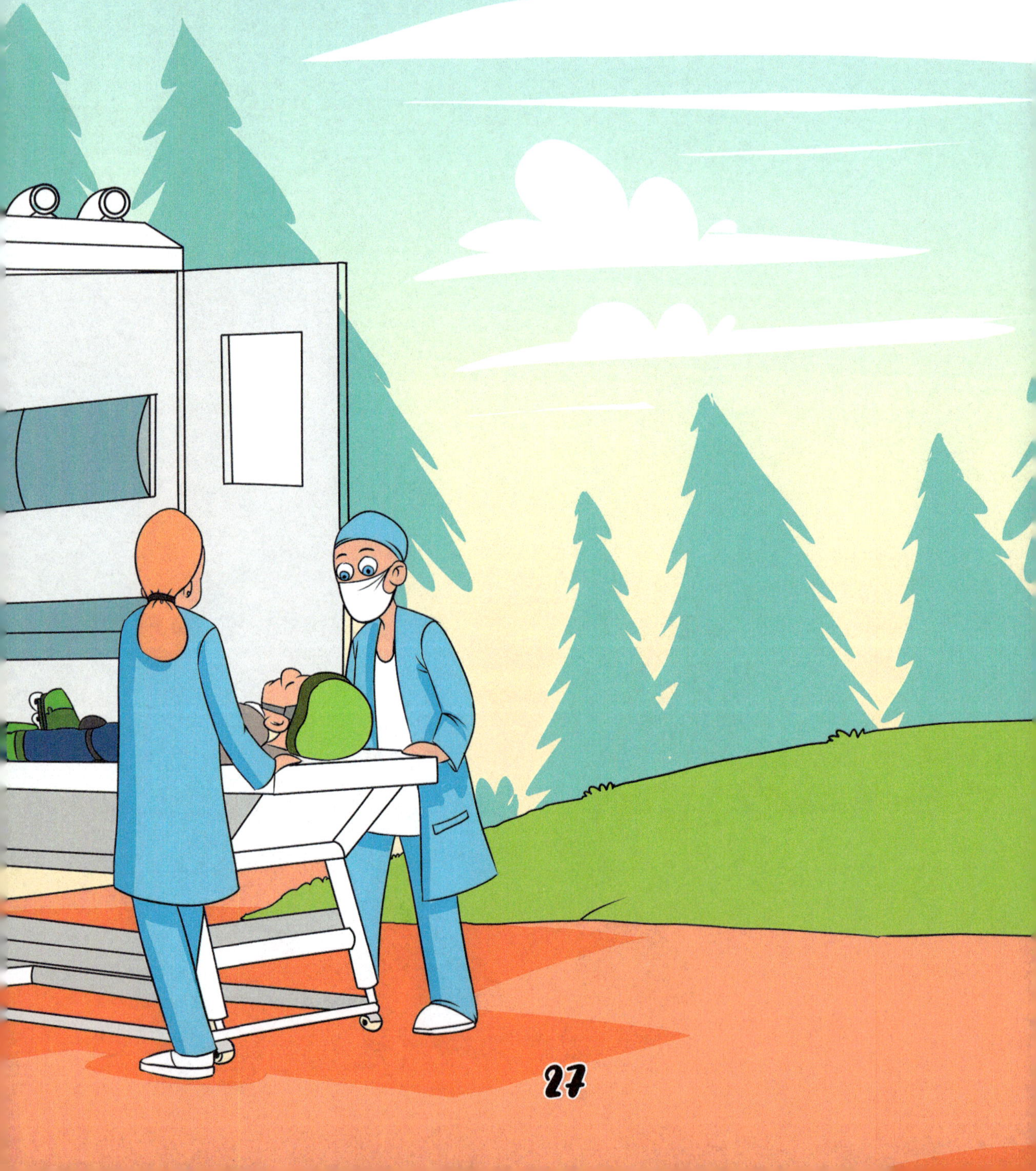

At the infirmary, Mrs. Karen, the school nurse, revealed to Ana and Tomy that Ryan was diabetic and he needed his insulin pen.

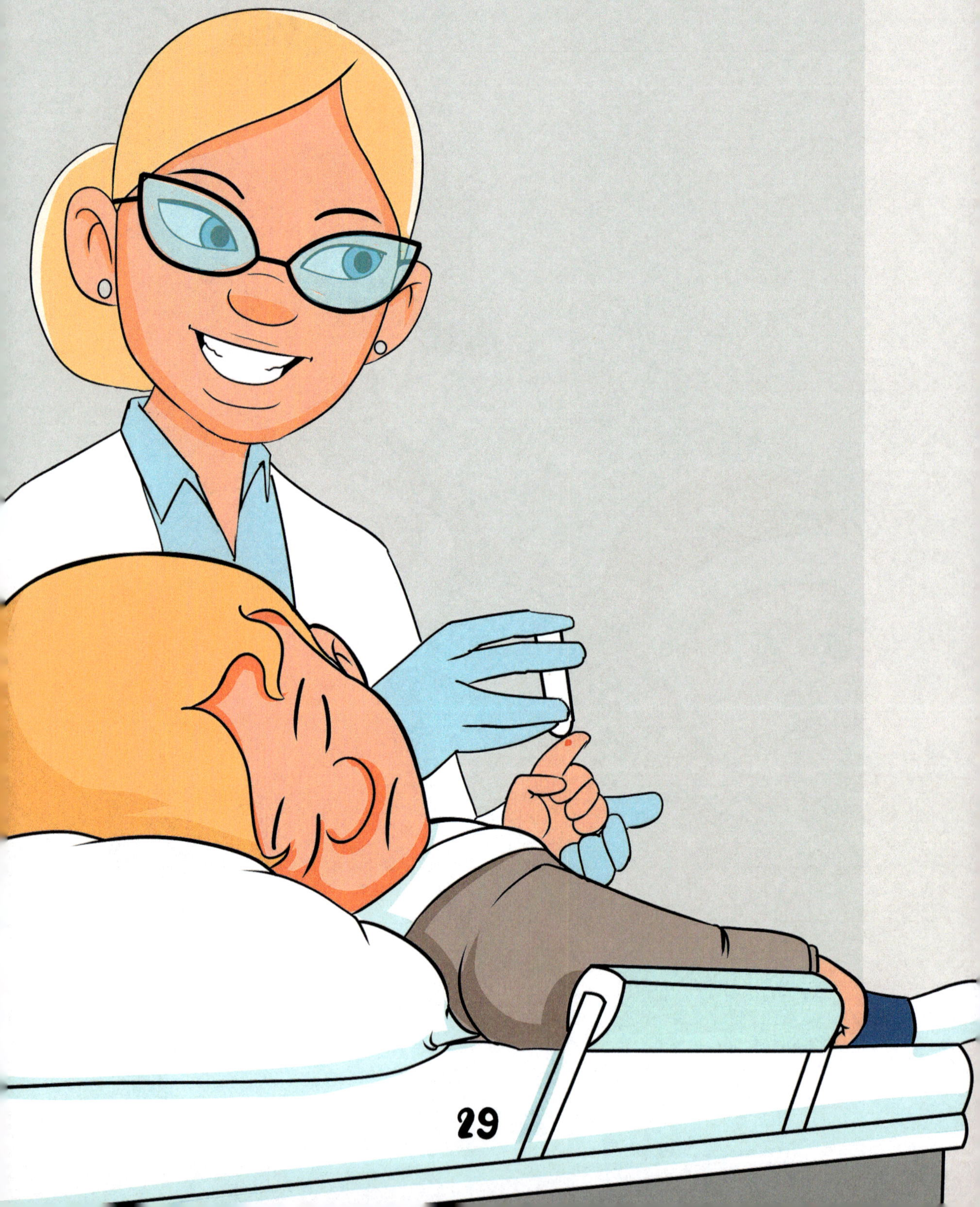

She said:"**Your friend is diabetic. He's going to be fine if you quickly find his insulin pen.**"

"Kids, let me explain to you something about Ryan's Type 1 Diabetes.
Our body needs energy from the food we eat. The pancreas creates insulin to allow the sugar from the food to enter our cells and gives us that energy.
The problem with Ryan is that his pancreas does not produce enough insulin. " Dr. Karen said.

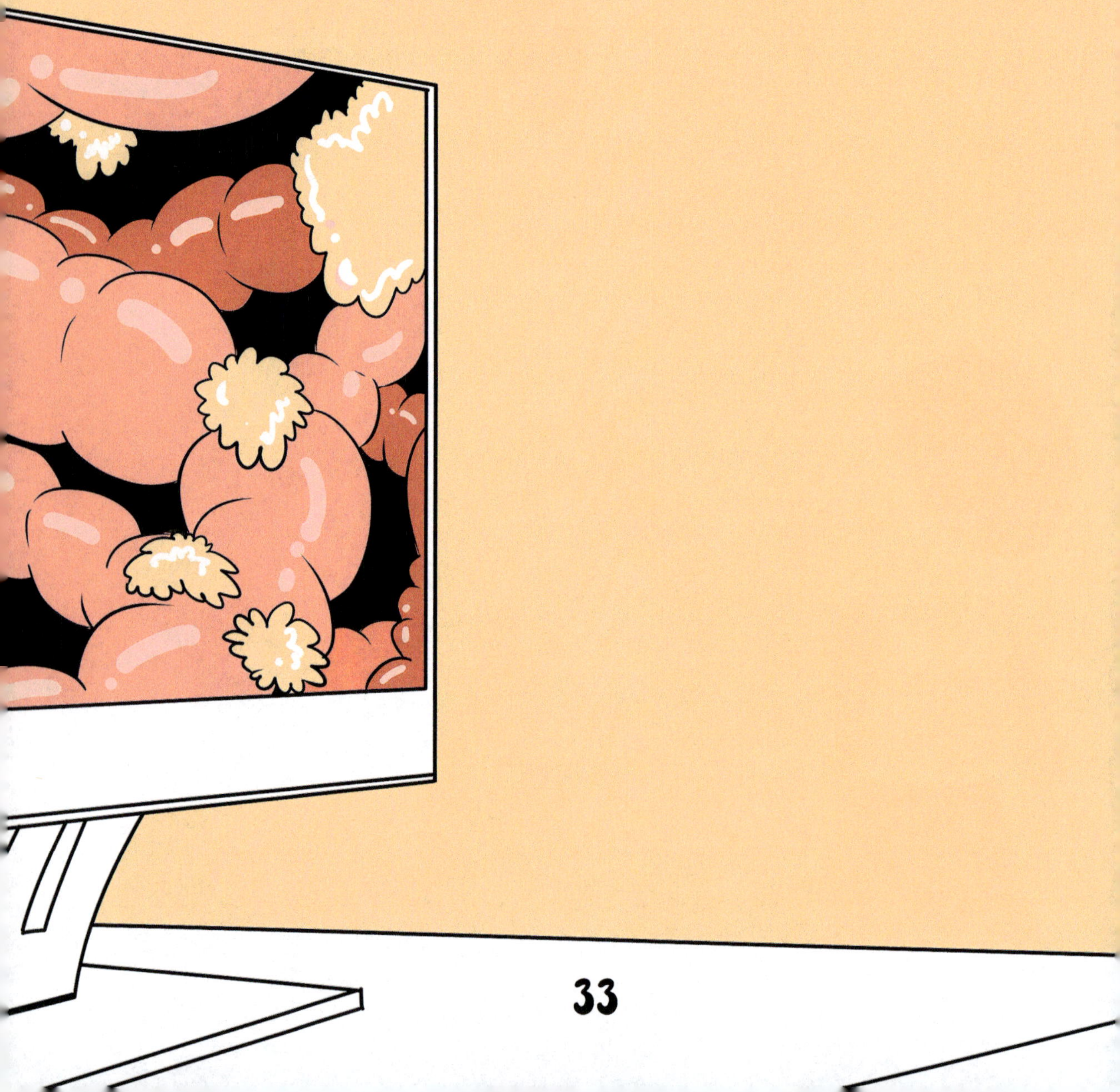

"**That's why he felt tired, and weak.**" Tomy replied.

"**...and he was also always hungry.**" Ana added.

SUPERKIDS. ASSEMBLE!

LET'S FIGHT THE DISEASE!

When the superkids arrived in Ryan's pancreas, Ana said to her brother Tomy:

"Look Tomy, Mummy was right! There is little insulin in his pancreas."

"**Without Insulin, the sugar from his food stays in his bloodstream.**" She added.

"**Is it bad?**" Tomy asked.

"**Yes, high blood sugar is damaging to the body.** " Ana replied.

"**What can we do, Ana? We need to save Ryan.**" Tommy said.

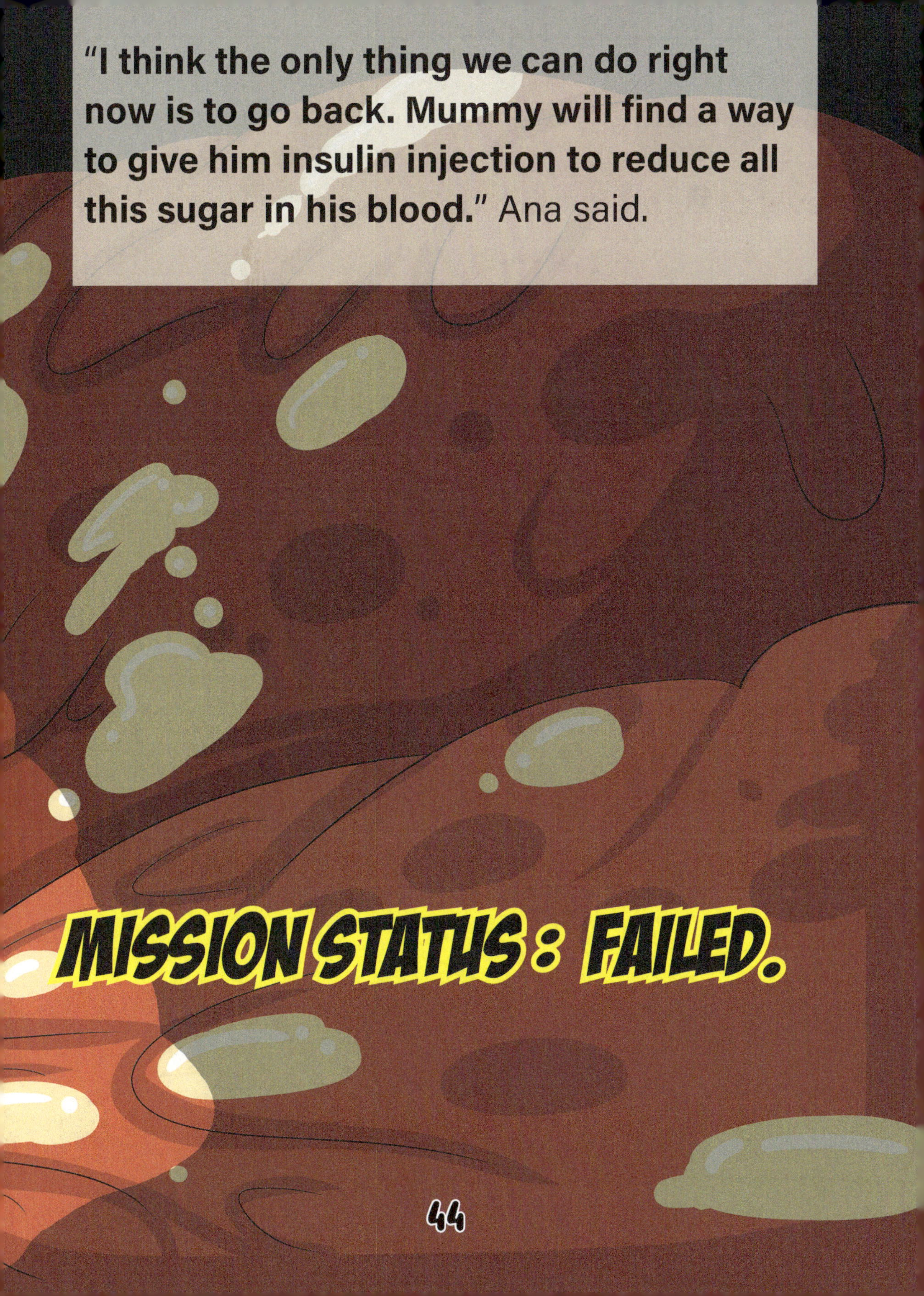
"I think the only thing we can do right now is to go back. Mummy will find a way to give him insulin injection to reduce all this sugar in his blood." Ana said.
MISSION STATUS : FAILED.

Ana and Tomy returned from their mission, and they were very disappointed.

"**Sorry Mummy, we went to the pancreas to check his insulin level and we also saw the high level of sugar in his bloodstream.**" Ana said.

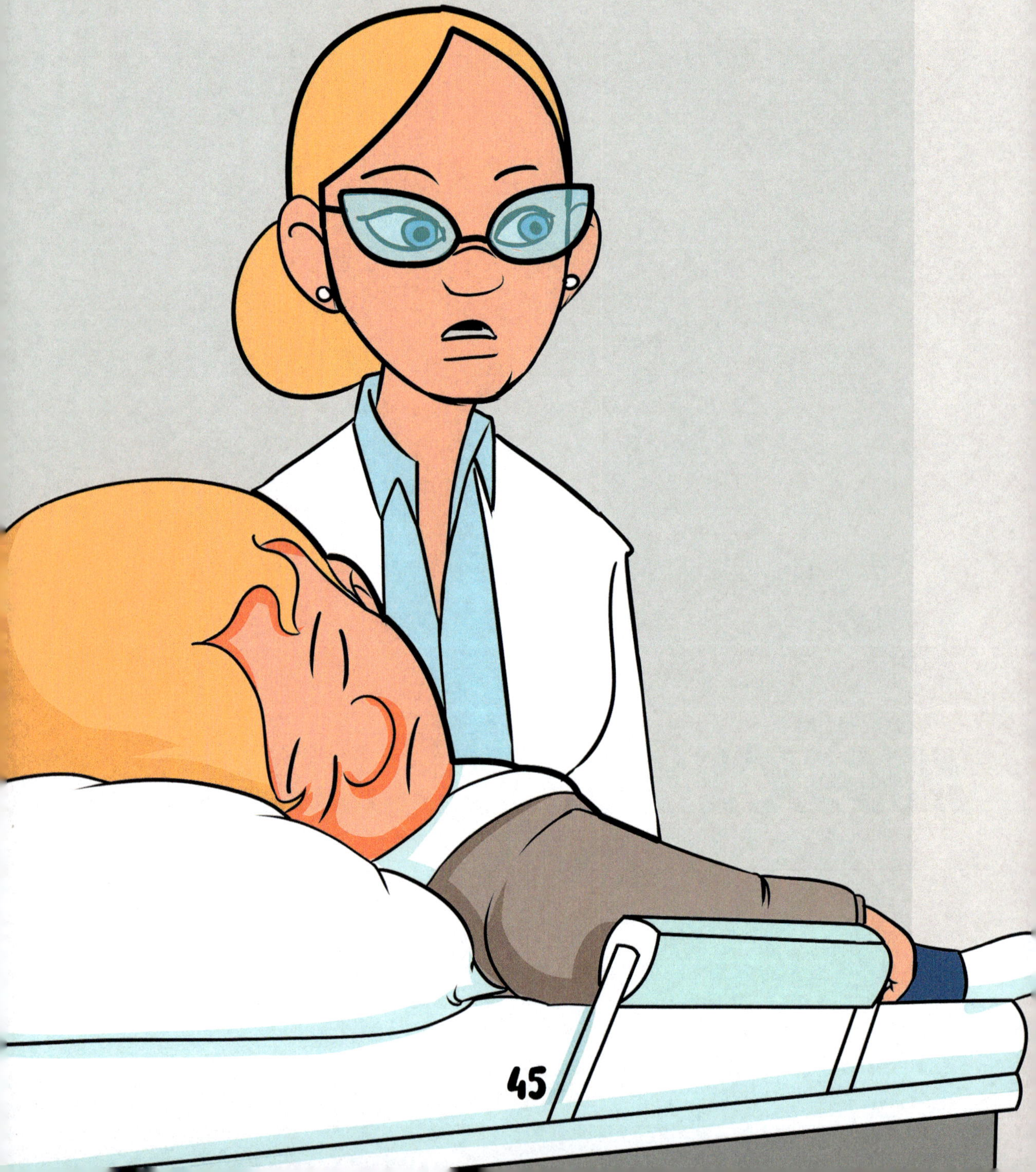

"**We failed. We could not help him, and we are going to lose our race against Terry**" Tomy added.

Mr. Fields announced the final race.

"**Kids, we will have our final race. Unfortunately, Ryan is still at the infirmary. Ana, your team is disqualified.**" said the P.E. teacher.

While Tomy was sad, Ana found the insulin pen in Russ's bag.

Ana rushed to the infirmary to give Ryan his insulin Pen.

Ryan injected his insulin and felt better.
He was ready to compete.

Mr. Fields announced the start of the final race.

Ready ... Set ... Go!

Ana, Tomy and Ryan won easily against Terry, Russ, and Zoe.

All the kids celebrated with them.

Mrs. Karen came to the class to educate the kids about Type 1 diabetes, its symptoms and its treatments.

She also talked about the role of insulin and glucose.

Cerebrovascular disease
Retinopathy and Blindness
Permanent kidney damage

After the lesson on Type 1 Diabetes by Mrs. Karen, only vegetables and fruits were served at the canteen to improve children good nutrition and health.

Terry and Russ did not look very happy about that.

TYPE 1 DIABETES KEY INFORMATION

Type 1 diabetes, once known as juvenile diabetes or insulin-dependent diabetes, is a chronic condition. In this condition, the pancreas makes little or no insulin. Insulin is a hormone the body uses to allow sugar (glucose) to enter cells to produce energy.

Different factors, such as genetics and some viruses, may cause type 1 diabetes. Although type 1 diabetes usually appears during childhood or adolescence, it can develop in adults.

Symptoms

Type 1 diabetes symptoms can appear suddenly and may include:

- Feeling more thirsty than usual
- Urinating a lot
- Bed-wetting in children who have never wet the bed during the night
- Feeling very hungry
- Losing weight without trying
- Feeling irritable or having other mood changes
- Feeling tired and weak
- Having blurry vision

Always Hungry
Always Tired
Increased Thirst
Frequent Urination
Nausea
Blurry Vision
Sudden Weight Loss
Sexual Problems
Slow Healing of Wounds

The role of glucose

Glucose — a sugar — is a main source of energy for the cells that make up muscles and other tissues.

- Glucose comes from two major sources: food and the liver.
- Sugar is absorbed into the bloodstream, where it enters cells with the help of insulin.
- The liver stores glucose in the form of glycogen.
- When glucose levels are low, such as when you haven't eaten in a while, the liver breaks down the stored glycogen into glucose. This keeps glucose levels within a typical range.

In type 1 diabetes, there's no insulin to let glucose into the cells. Because of this, sugar builds up in the bloodstream. This can cause life-threatening complications.

Risk factors

Some factors that can raise your risk for type 1 diabetes include:

Diabetes

Testing Blood

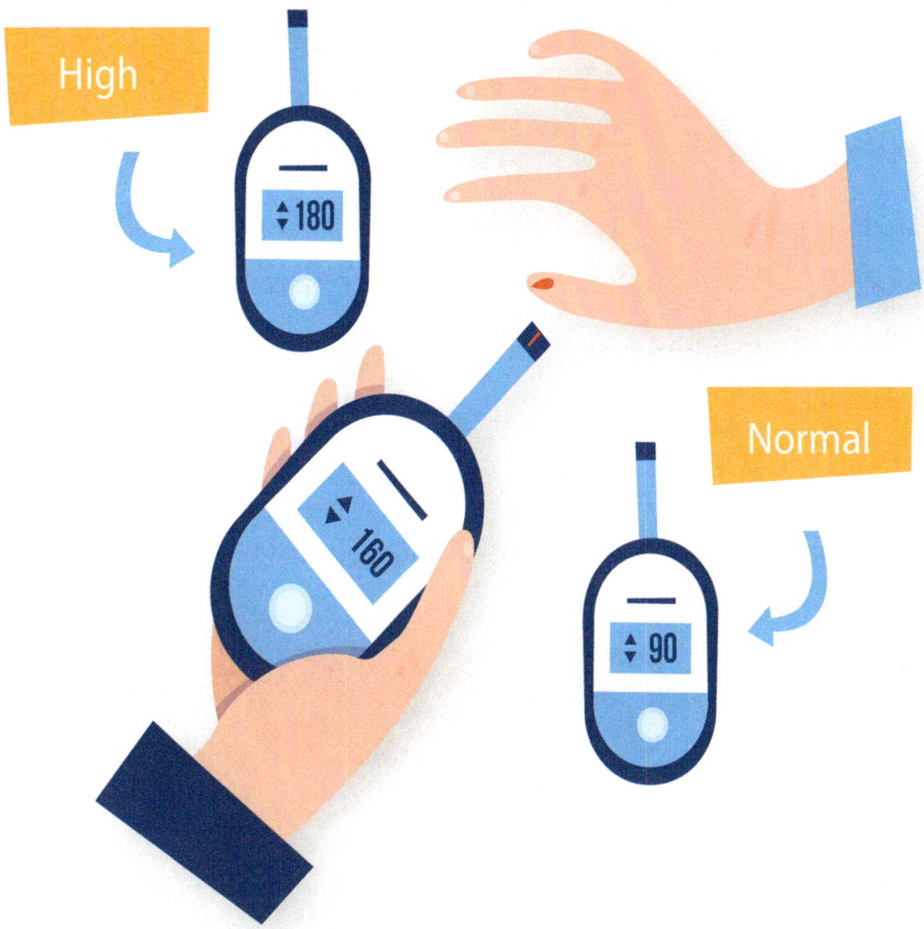

- Family history. Anyone with a parent or sibling with type 1 diabetes has a slightly higher risk of developing the condition.
- Genetics. Having certain genes increases the risk of developing type 1 diabetes.
- Geography. The number of people who have type 1 diabetes tends to be higher as you travel away from the equator.
- Age. Type 1 diabetes can appear at any age, but it appears at two noticeable peaks. The first peak occurs in children between 4 and 7 years old. The second is in children between 10 and 14 years old.

Causes

The exact cause of type I diabetes is unknown. Usually, the body's own immune system — which normally fights harmful bacteria and viruses — destroys the insulin-producing (islet) cells in the pancreas. Other possible causes include:

- Genetics
- Exposure to viruses and other environmental factors

The role of insulin

Once a large number of islet cells are destroyed, the body will produce little or no insulin. Insulin is a hormone that comes from a gland behind and below the stomach (pancreas).

- The pancreas puts insulin into the bloodstream.
- Insulin travels through the body, allowing sugar to enter the cells.
- Insulin lowers the amount of sugar in the bloodstream.
- As the blood sugar level drops, the pancreas puts less insulin into the bloodstream.

COMPLICATIONS:

Permanent Kidney Damage

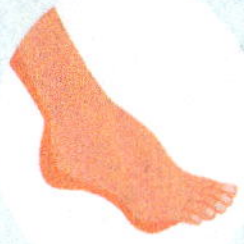
Diabetic Foot

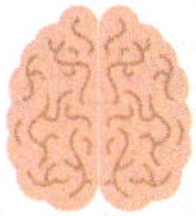
Cerebrovascular Diseases

Peripheral Neuropathy

Eye Damage

Coronary Heart Disease

TREATMENT:

Diabetes Medications

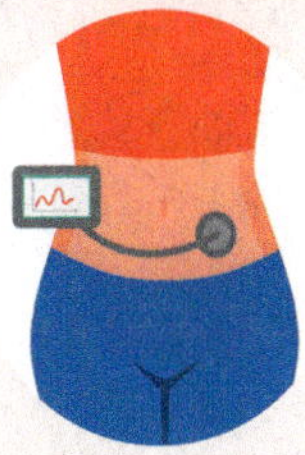
Blood Sugar Monitoring

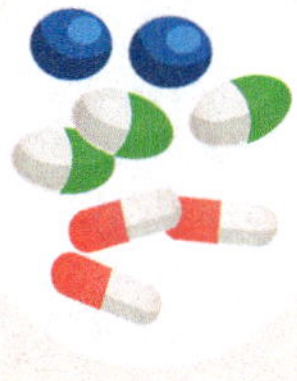
Insulin Pills

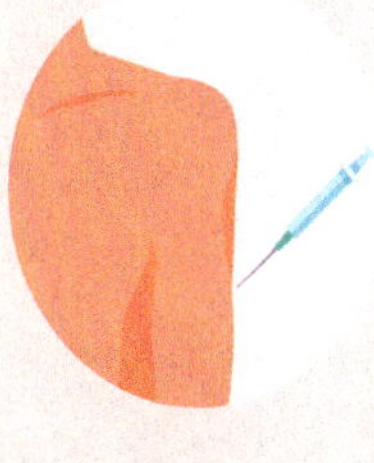
Insulin Injections

AUTHORS BIO

Born in France, Raised in Cameroon. Studied in United Kingdom and Canada. Married a Congolese and travel to more than 50 different countries in the world. Patrick is a travel enthusiast and a people lover. So much so that since he became a father, his only focus is to transmit (without success yet) that gene to his kids (Wellysane, Ywaika and Janea Kymia). By the way, the children books of the Superkids Adventures Series are first and foremost for them. If you read it, consider yourself lucky. So, Enjoy without restriction.

Philip PATMAN - The Writer

From the motherland Ghana with Love. I am Mike, The one, only and Undisputed Comics. I am a lot of things all together. Concept artist, Comics fanatic, Creative, independent, and detail-oriented graphic designer with multiple years of experience in digital brand management, logo design, illustrations, storyboards, Character development and layout design. Highly skilled with Adobe Photoshop and Illustrator Coachable and passionate about collaborating with a team when working on projects. My ultimate dream is to create an iconic character or comic that will be read by people all around the World. Undisputed.

Michael OFORI - The Illustrator

My name is Delphine Shooter and I am a digital illustrator.
My love for art stemmed from my interest in human features and animated films. I started with making doodles at the back of my notebooks to making short illustrated stories and posting them on my social media pages.
My goal is to work at top animation studios around the world and probably even set up my own studio for creating children's books. There is so much I am looking forward to learning to become the best professional artist I can be.

Delphine SHOOTER - The Designer

1 2 3

8 13 21 34 55 89

Printed in Great Britain
by Amazon

30782018R00044